Witch Craft

Wicked Accessories, Creepy-Cute Toys,
Magical Treats, and More!

Compiled by

MARGARET MCGUIRE *and* ALICIA KACHMAR

QUIRK BOOKS
PHILADELPHIA

Library of Congress Cataloging in Publication Number: 9781594744860

ISBN: 978-1-59474-486-0

Printed in China

Typeset in Mr. Eaves, Mrs. Eaves, Bookman Swash, Trade Gothic

Designed by Sugar
Photography by Steve Belkowitz except pages 17, 18, 37, 38, 54, 55, 69
by Maki Ogawa and pages 26, 27 by Robyn Lee
Production management by John J. McGurk

Distributed in North America by Chronicle Books
680 Second Street
San Francisco, CA 94107

10 9 8 7 6 5 4 3 2 1

Quirk Books
215 Church Street
Philadelphia, PA 19106
www.irreference.com
www.quirkbooks.com

Contents

Introduction: What Lurks Within   5

Witchy Stitches: Sewing, Crocheting
   & Knitting Basics   6

Metric Conversions   8

The Witch Crafts

Bewitching Headbands & Corsages   10

Bottled Potions: Love Potions, Dragon's Blood, Wolfsbane,
   Lucky Stars, Flying Potions & More   13

Chocolate Marshmallow Skulls   17

Creepy Crocheted Bones   19

Cross-Stitch Witch & Friends   21

Crystal Balls, Spell Jars & Snow Globes   24

Cupcake Graveyard   26

Dracula's Candy Bowl   28

Freaky Finger Food   31

Fuzzy Bats   33

Ghost Toasts   37

Good Little Witch   39

Halloween Cupcake Toppers   42

Knitted Spider & Spiderweb Hat   45

Lovely Wicked Tutus 48

Magical Catnapping Mask 51

Peanut Butter & Jelly Skull Sandwiches 54

Plushie Poison Apples 56

Poison Ivy Lip Embellishment 59

Ruby Slippers 61

Sleepy Ghost Brooches 63

Spider Earrings 66

Tangerine Jack-o'-Lanterns 69

Trick-or-Treat Garlands 71

Vampire Bite Necklaces 73

Wicked Mary-Janes: Zombie Kittens,
    Dracula vs. Frankenstein & More 75

Witches' Brew 78

About the Witch Crafters 80

Dark Arts & Crafts Shopping Guide 93

Acknowledgments 95

Introduction:

WHAT LURKS WITHIN

VELCOME!

Within this little book of *Witch Craft* you'll find the secret to crafting simple homemade tricks and treats to delight your family and friends.

Refashion old glass jars of all shapes and sizes into sparkly homemade crystal balls, spell jars, and snow globes.

Stitch up leftover fabric and a pretty ribbon into a bewitching headband in minutes!

Transform tangerines and oranges into tiny, edible jack-o'-lanterns.

Each step-by-step project is as easy as the tap of a wand! These simple supplies help transform everyday items into magical, witchy crafts:

• scissors	• yarn
• needle and thread	• fabric, such as silk, felt, and lace
• stuffing, such as fiberfill, cotton batting, or fabric scraps	• needle-nose pliers
	• pencil and tracing paper
• knitting needles	• glitter
• crochet hook	• glue

A handy Dark Arts & Crafts Shopping Guide (page 93) is chock-full of crafting resources, so beginners and experts alike will be inspired to share in the fun. Creepy-cute toys, enchanting accessories, and tasty treats are just minutes away!

Witchy Stitches:

SEWING, CROCHETING & KNITTING BASICS

Sewing projects within this book can be stitched by hand or with the aid of a sewing machine. If you're new to sewing, crocheting, or knitting, Martha Stewart (Marthastewart.com), Crafty Daisies (Craftydaisies.com) and Knitting Help (Knittinghelp.com) feature excellent video tutorials, and books like *Martha Stewart's Encyclopedia of Crafts*, *Teach Yourself Visually Crocheting*, and *Teach Yourself Visually Knitting* are helpful resources when learning the basics. Video tutorials and in-depth features on the projects in this book can be found online at Irreference.com/Witch-Craft. All crochet and knitting projects in this book are written in American English and use the following terms and abbreviations.

SEWING TERMS

nap	the lay of the pile of the fabric
reverse	the back side of the fabric
selvage	the self-finished edges of fabric
seam allowance	the area between the edge and the stitching line

CROCHET ABBREVIATIONS

ch	chain
sc	single crochet
sl st	slip stitch
st	stitch
inc	increase (work 2 stitches into same space)
dec	decrease (draw up loops in next 2 stitches, yarn over and draw through all 3 loops on hook)

KNITTING ABBREVIATIONS

K	knit
P	purl
CO	cast on
Kf&b	knit into the front and back of stitch
yo	yarn over
K2tog	knit 2 together
K3tog	knit 3 together
skp	slip, knit, pass slip stitch over (single decrease)
NPS	Navajo ply stranding
M1L	From the front, lift the loop that lies between stitches with the left needle, then knit into the back of the loop
M1R	From the back, lift the loop that lies between stitches with the left needle, then knit (or purl, as in double knitting) into the front of the loop

Metric Conversions

VOLUME

U.S.	METRIC	U.S.	METRIC
¼ tsp	1.25 ml	⅓ cup	80 ml
½ tsp	2.5 ml	½ cup	120 ml
1 tsp	5 ml	1 cup	240 ml
1 tbsp (3 tsp)	15 ml	1 pint (2 cups)	480 ml
1 fl oz (2 tbsp)	30 ml	1 quart (2 pints)	960 ml
¼ cup	60 ml	1 gallon (4 quarts)	3.84 l

WEIGHT

U.S.	METRIC	U.S.	METRIC
1 oz	28 g	12 oz (¾ lb)	340 g
4 oz (¼ lb)	113 g	16 oz (1 lb)	454 g
8 oz (½ lb)	227 g	2.2 lb	1 kg

LENGTH

U.S.	METRIC	U.S.	METRIC
¼ in	0.65 cm	6 in	15.0 cm
½ in	1.25 cm	7 in	17.5 cm
1 in	2.50 cm	8 in	20.5 cm
2 in	5.00 cm	9 in	23.0 cm
3 in	7.50 cm	10 in	25.5 cm
4 in	10.0 cm	12 in	30.5 cm
5 in	12.5 cm	15 in	38.0 cm

Bewitching Headbands & Corsages

Fashion silk and ribbon into headbands, corsages, or belts
adorned with midnight black rosebuds.

by RACHEL SAUVAGEOT

supplies

- scissors

- about ¼ yard thin lining fabric, such as black china silk and black silk chiffon; or about ⅛ yard for a wrist corsage, ½ yard for a belt

- about ⅛ yard metallic tulle

- about 36 inches ribbon for a headband; or about 2 yards for a belt, 20 inches for a wrist corsage

- needle and thread

1. Use scissors or a rotary cutter to cut fabric into about 100 2½-inch squares, such as 60 squares of china silk, 20 squares of silk chiffon, and 20 squares of tulle.

2. Trim corners to make squares into circles; you can stack the squares and cut several layers at once to save time. They don't have to be perfect, since imperfections won't show once you're done.

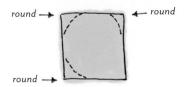

round → ← round

round →

Cutting is fast and easy with the help of a rotary cutter, cutting mat, and metal ruler or straight edge. See page 93 for where to purchase them.

EEEK!

3. Put a circle of tulle or chiffon on top of a circle of silk; set aside. Fold a silk circle in half and then in half again, making a triangular bud shape.

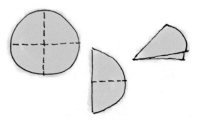

4. Put folded tip in the center of the first circle of silk and tulle. Fold silk and tulle around it to make a triangle, the folded edges forming the point and a nice, full ruffly edge at the end.

5. Starting in the middle of ribbon, sew on tip of triangle with a few stitches. Check that you're sewing through all the layers but leaving ruffled ends free.

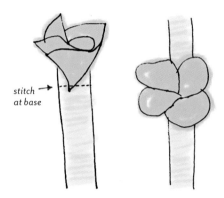

stitch at base →

Sew rows close together for a thick, full effect or space them apart for a more delicate look. Simply cut the circles larger for huge, loose blossoms or smaller for dainty little petals.

6. For wrist corsage, sew on triangular buds in a single row; for headband or belt, sew them in rows of two or three for a lush, full look.

7. Make triangular buds out of all circles and stitch them to ribbon.

Flower-bud edges are left unfinished, which means you can't just toss your headband in the washer without the risk of serious unraveling. But it's a headband, after all, so hopefully it won't need heavy-duty cleaning.

Bottled Potions

With this special recipe, you can bottle and carry love potions,
magical dragon's blood, wolfsbane, antidotes, shimmery lucky stars,
and flying potions, or your own special concoctions!

by CAROL LIN

- wire cutters and needle-nose pliers
- 20-gauge jewelry wire (about 5 inches per bottle)
- liquid potion or lucky stars (pages 15 to 16) or other tiny treasures of your choosing
- bottles and corks
- paper or stickers for labels

(1) Cut a 5-inch piece of wire. If you'd like an accessory loop, use pliers to twist it twice into a tight curl about 2 inches from one end so it'll face out when you hang your bottled pendant from a ribbon.

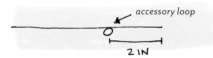

accessory loop

2 IN

(2) Wrap wire around bottle neck.

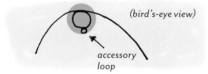

(bird's-eye view)

accessory loop

(3) Straighten ends into a right angle. With pliers, bend longer end into a tear-drop-shape loop.

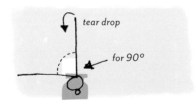

tear drop

for 90°

(4) Coil shorter end around base of loop 3 to 6 times. Trim excess wire if necessary. Bend loop upward so that it makes a good pendant.

pendant

(5) Fill bottle with a liquid potion (page 15), flying potion or lucky stars (page 16), or other tiny treasures!

(6) For handmade labels, write the name of your potion onto pieces of paper. Affix them to bottles with glue. Or use store-bought sticker labels.

Tiny origami stars, pretty beads, and other charms can be threaded onto wire and secured to accessory loops.

LOVE POTION: Mix pink cake shimmer into your potion to capture your beloved's heart.

DRAGON'S BLOOD: Add extra red food coloring to carry the protective magic of Dragon's Blood with you everywhere.

WOLFSBANE POTION: Add green food coloring to your potion to ward off werewolves.

- cake shimmer and water
- 1 pinch salt for every 2 millimeters (or 1 tablespoon for every 4 ounces)
- food coloring (optional)
- a few drops glycerin

1. In a bowl, mix water and cake shimmer with a paintbrush. Mix in salt and glycerin, which will thicken mixture and help suspend sparkling cake shimmer. Then add food coloring, if desired.

2. Using a pipette or funnel, fill bottles with potion. Seal with corks.

Cake shimmer comes in a rainbow of colors (see page 93), and you can mix silver or white cake shimmer with diluted food coloring to create your own hues.

ANTIDOTE: Combine water and green food coloring to reach desired hue. Fill bottle two-thirds with mixture and top with a few drops olive or other cooking oil for a two-tone effect. Keep a bottle on hand to reverse any curse imaginable!

Add oil after colored water so that it sits on the surface instead of clinging to the sides of the bottle.

EEEK!

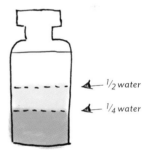

— 1/2 water

— 1/4 water

Use a 1:1 ratio of water to cake shimmer for transparent potions. Use a 1:3 ratio for dark, vibrant potions.

For flying potions, fill bottles with colorful feathers trimmed to fit. For years of good fortune brought on by shimmery lucky stars, you can purchase tiny origami stars or make your own.

EEEK!

LUCKY STARS

Origami paper strips can be purchased in craft stores and online (see page 93 for where to find them). They're typically $^1/_4$ inch wide by 5 $^7/_8$ inches long and come in shimmery, neon, patterned, or even glow-in-the-dark styles.

1. Use scissors or a utility knife and metal ruler to make paper strips even smaller (2 to 5 millimeters by 6 to 7 millimeters). Variation in size is okay, since you need only one strip to make a star.

2. Fold a knot toward the end of one strip. Tuck in short end to make a pentagon shape, with one short end and one long end.

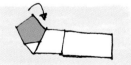

3. Fold short and long ends around the valleys of the pentagon.

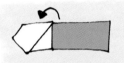

4. When they're too small to keep folding, tuck into pentagon.

5. Using your fingers, pinch in all five corners to puff your star. Done!

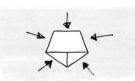

Chocolate Marshmallow Skulls

Drawing with chocolate frosting is a fun way to transform marshmallows into eerie skulls! Perfect for sharing mugs of hot cocoa with children and friends on a chilly autumn night.

by MAKI OGAWA

supplies

- marshmallows
- knife
- pastry bag or condiment pencil (optional)
- chocolate frosting

1. Arrange marshmallows on a cutting board.

2. Using a knife, gently cut each marshmallow in half and then score each one where you will draw the mouth.

3. With chocolate frosting, draw lines for mouths. Add hatch marks for teeth and dots for eyes and noses.

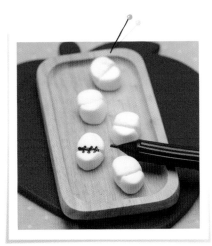

Boo! Float marshmallow skulls in hot cocoa for a spooky surprise. Use them along with colorful sprinkles to decorate ice-cream sundaes, cakes, or cupcakes.

You can draw with frosting that comes in a tube or use a pastry bag or condiment pencil (page 93) filled with homemade frosting!

Creepy Crocheted Bones

Gnarly crocheted bones can decorate your
kitchen table or stick out of your candy bowl!

by ALICIA KACHMAR

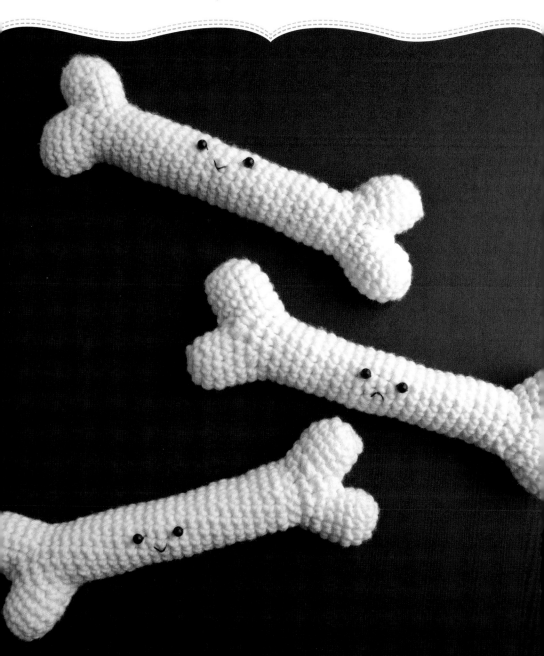

- G hook
- white worsted-weight yarn
- 2 (5- to 6-millimeter) black beads or buttons
- black embroidery thread and needle
- stuffing

1. **Round 1:** Ch 2; 6sc in 2nd ch from hook {6}. **Round 2:** [Inc] around {12}. **Round 3:** Sc around {12}. **Round 4:** Sc around and sl st to next stitch {12}. Fasten off. Repeat Rounds 1 through 4 again, but do not fasten off. Join the two pieces together with sc in each of next 2 sc.

2. **Round 5:** Sc around each piece, making a dec on each piece. Dec where the pieces are joined each time {20}. **Round 6:** Sc around each piece, making a dec on each piece. Dec where the pieces are joined each time {16}. **Round 7:** Sc around each piece, making a dec on each piece {14}.

3. Sc around for 24 more rounds and fasten off.

4. Repeat Steps 1 and 2 and fasten off, leaving a 12-inch tail for sewing.

5. Sew on bead or button eyes, positioning one each on the 18th and 22nd round of the first bone piece. Stitch mouth with embroidery thread. Stuff both pieces and sew the bone together.

Two quick stitches make a happy smile— or a grumpy frown!

Cross-Stitch Witch & Friends

Hand-stitched ghoulish jewelry is as easy as pumpkin pie.

by SAMANTHA PURDY

supplies

- fabric button cover kits
  (sizes 1 ½ centimeters and 1 ½ inches)
- needle-nose pliers
- even-weave embroidery fabric, such as Aida cloth
- embroidery hoop and thread in multiple colors, such as DMC in black, white, 954 (nile green), 606 (orange-red bright), 742 (tangerine light), and 947 (burnt orange)
- white tapestry yarn, needle, and thread
- 2 silver seed beads
- clasp pins or earring posts and backings
- strong adhesive, such as Gorilla glue

1 Use the circle guide from fabric button cover kit to determine the amount of fabric you'll need to cover each button. Using pliers, remove the button loop from the back of each button cover. Keep the back of the button to snap into place later.

2 Trace patterns onto fabric. Determine approximate center by folding circle lengthwise and widthwise; mark it with a pencil. Secure fabric in an embroidery hoop or cut an inch wider than needed so that you can grip it while stitching.

3 Start the design from the center out and switch colors as marked on pattern. **For witch:** Use one strand of white tapestry yarn for her hair; sew on 2 silver seed beads with needle and thread for the buttons on her cape.

4 Cut around finished circle and discard extra fabric. Use button cover tools or your fingers to pull fabric edges tightly around back of button. Check that design is centered. Snap back of each button into place.

5 Glue pins or earring posts to the backs; let dry overnight. Wipe earring backs with rubbing alcohol to clean.

Button cover kits can transform spooky cross-stitch projects into buttons, brooches, or earrings!

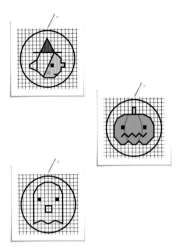

You can use tracing paper and chalk pencil to transfer these patterns or drawings of your own creepy critters onto fabric.

BROOCH PATTERN

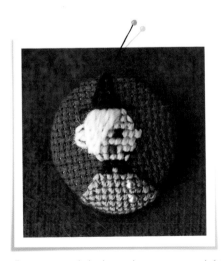

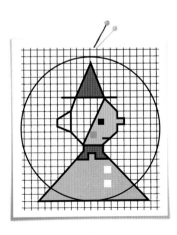

For a super spooky background, you can use purple fabric dye to turn white fabric a brilliant shade of blue-violet. For fabric dye and button cover kits, see page 93. Just make sure dyed fabric is thoroughly rinsed and dried before you start stitching.

Crystal Balls, Spell Jars & Snow Globes

Transform old or new glass jars into sparkling crystal balls!
Seal in glitter and plastic spiders or other creepy crawlies.

by SHALET ABRAHAM

- clean glass jar with a well-sealing lid
- small store-bought or homemade toys or figurines that fit inside
- silicone glue or hot glue
- a few drops glycerin
- glitter
- felt and ribbon to decorate

1) Glue plastic figurines to jar's interior; let dry overnight.

2) Fill jar three-fourths with distilled water. Add glycerin. (Note: the more you use, the clumpier your glitter will be.) Add glitter and eyeballs (see below), plastic spiders, or other toys that you want to float, and fill jar to the brim with water.

3) Over a sink, put lid on the jar and check that you like how it looks. Remove lid and coat its inside edge with glue. Add more water if needed. Keeping jar upright, seal lid tightly and let glue dry overnight.

Glycerin can be found in the baking supply section of grocery or craft stores. It magically slows glitter's movement in water!

4) Test integrity of seal. If it leaks, add a small bead of glue on the lid's outside edge. Let dry thoroughly.

5) Cut a piece of felt to dimensions of bottom of lid and glue in place. Glue or tie ribbon around the edge for a pretty finish.

It's easy to make floaty eyeballs out of recycled materials. With a flathead screwdriver, pry the roller ball from an empty roll-on deodorant container. Wash and dry. Use acrylic paint to transform it into a bloodshot eyeball. Let dry between coats. Finish with a coat of clear spray-on acrylic sealer. Let dry overnight.

Cupcake Graveyard

You'll kill off these cupcakes in no time.

by GRACE HIURA

supplies

- ¼ cup semisweet chocolate chips
- ½ teaspoon vegetable oil
- I sandwich-size plastic bag
- kitchen scissors
- I2 cookies
- I (I6-ounce) container vanilla frosting
- about I5 drops green food coloring
- I2 cupcakes, cooled and unfrosted

1. Combine chocolate chips and oil in a small microwave-safe bowl, and heat at 50 percent power for 30 seconds; stir and repeat. Stir until chips are melted and mixture is smooth. Pour into a corner of the plastic bag.

2. **For tombstones:** Snip off a tiny piece of the bag's corner and work melted chocolate toward the opening. Pipe "RIP" or other decoration onto the upper third of each cookie so that it'll be visible when cookie is pushed into cupcake. Let stand 30 minutes at room temperature, or until chocolate sets.

3. In a bowl, combine frosting with food coloring. Frost cupcakes and insert cookie tombstones. Decorate with plastic toys, gummy worms, chocolate mushrooms, and other treats.

For spiky grass, tap frosted cupcakes with the tip of a dinner knife. For long grass, pipe frosting onto cupcakes. For dirt cupcakes, add crushed chocolate cookie crumbs to chocolate frosting. To decorate chocolate cookies, use melted white chocolate chips instead of semisweet.

EEEK!

Plastic decorations like bats, spiders, black cats can be found in craft stores or online, and spooky edible embellishments like chocolate mushrooms, gummy worms, and frogs are sold in grocery stores. See page 93 for ideas.

Dracula's Candy Bowl

Count Dracula has a sweet tooth! To stave off vicious cravings,
fill this felted knit candy bowl to the brim with tricks and treats.

by FLOSSIE AREND

supplies

- about 1 skein each black (AC), white (TC), red (MC), and silvery blue or gray (FC) worsted-weight yarn such as Patons classic 100% wool in black, aran, that's red, and Sheperd classic 100% wool in cloud

- size 13 circular knitting needles

- 38-inch magic loop or 13 double-pointed needles

- size M crochet hook (or any size larger than J)

- at least 3 knitting bobbins

- bowl or coffee can for molding, about 4½ inches wide and 6½ inches tall

For step-by-step videos detailing this project, visit Irreference.com/Witch-Craft.

EEEK!

BOWL

1. Make one slipknot with red yarn. Pull working end through it for a working 3-stranded length of yarn. As you work, continue pulling working yarn through the loop to keep 3 strands. This is called Navajo ply stranding method (NPS).

2. Make a loop around your finger so that your working yarn falls to the left behind it. Insert crochet hook under loop, grab working yarn, and pull through. Without going through loop a second time, hook working yarn and pull through loop on crochet hook. Continue for 10 stitches. This is called Emily Ocker's circular cast-on.

3. Use these stitches to make a magic loop: Carefully transfer them to circular needles. Divide stitches between needles, pulling circular needle cord between them for 5 stitches on each needle.

4. Keep working yarn needle in your right hand: Move off these stitches backward onto the cord, leaving needle bare. When stitches are worked, a loop of cord will lie on either end.

5. Once you have worked a few rounds, pull loose end to close the hole.

6. **Round 1:** Knit all odd rounds. **Round 2:** Kf&b all stitches (20 sts). **Round 4:** *Kf&b, K1, repeat from * around (30 sts). **Round 6:** *Kf&b, K2, repeat from * around (40 sts). **Round 8:** *Kf&b, K3, repeat from * around (50 sts). **Round 10:** *Kf&b, K4, repeat from * around (60 sts). **Rounds 11 to 12:** Knit. Using 2 55-inch pieces white yarn (TC). Create a triple strand with each using NPS and wrap both around 2 bobbins for the teeth. **Round 13:** K8(MC), K1(TC), K11(MC), K1(TC), K39(MC). **Round 14:** K7(MC), K3(TC), K9(MC), K3(TC), K38(MC). **Round 15:** K7(MC), K3(TC), K9(MC), K3(TC), K38(MC). Measure about 100 inches

red yarn (MC). Create a triple strand using NPS and wrap around a bobbin for the mouth. **Round 16**: K5(MC), K19(FC), K36(MC). **Rounds 17 to 19**: K60(MC). Unwind (FC) yarn from bobbins and weave in ends with tapestry needle. Measure about 48 inches black (AC) yarn. Create a triple strand using NPS and wrap around a bobbin for the nose. **Round 20**: K12(MC), K5(AC), K43(MC). **Round 21**: K12(MC), K1(AC), K3(MC), K1(AC), K43(MC). **Rounds 22 and 23**: K60(MC). Measure out 2 50-inch pieces red yarn (FC). Make both into triple strands using NPS and wrap both around 2 bobbins for Dracula's eyes. Join the skein of black yarn into remaining knit rounds, create a triple-strand using NPS, and carry through behind the work. **Round 24**: K3(AC),

K6(MC), K3(FC), K5 (MC), K3(FC), K6(MC), K3(AC), K31(MC). **Round 25**: K2(AC), K7(MC), K3(FC), K1(AC), K3(MC), K1(AC), K3(FC), K7(MC), K2(AC), K31(MC). **Round 26**: K1(AC), K5(MC), K2(AC), K2(MC), K1(FC), K1(AC), K5(MC), K1(AC), K1(FC), K2(MC), K2(AC), K5(MC), K32(AC). **Round 27**: K1(AC), K6(MC), K4(AC), K7(MC), K4(AC), K6(MC), K32(AC). **Rounds 28 to 29**: K1(AC), K13(MC), K1(AC), K13(MC), K32(AC). **Round 30**: K2(AC), K11(MC), K3(AC), K11(MC), K33(AC). **Round 31**: K3(AC), K9(MC), K5(AC), K9(MC), K34(AC). **Round 32**: K4(AC), K7(MC), K7(AC), K7(MC), K35(AC). **Round 33**: K60(AC). Bind off all stitches.

FELTING

7 Place bowl into a pillowcase and felt with detergent in the first cycle of a hot wash in a top-loading washing machine. Repeat if necessary, but check shape every few minutes.

8 Roll into a towel and squeeze out excess water. Put molding bowl inside and let sit for 2 to 3 days. When dry, remove molding bowl. *Voila!*

To make a handsome cape for Dracula, download the free cape pattern PDF: Irreference.com/Witch-Craft!

Freaky Finger Food

Hand over those carrots…if you dare!

by ALICIA KACHMAR

supplies

- bowl of your favorite dip (see recipe below)
- assorted vegetable sticks, such as carrots and celery
- sliced almonds

1. With a butter knife, spread a small amount of dip on the top of a vegetable stick.

2. Attach the flat side of an almond to the dip.

3. Repeat these steps for four more vegetable sticks.

4. Arrange in bowl of dip to resemble a hand, with the thumb and pinky finger pushed farther down and the middle finger standing the highest.

This tasty, nutritious treat is quick and easy to make. You can use carrots and celery or sesame sticks and pretzel rods with guacamole or spicy cheese dip.

ONION BEAN DIP

FROM THE CAULDRON OF WITCH E. WITCH

1 cup fresh parsley leaves

2 (16-ounce) cans cannellini
    beans, drained and rinsed

4 tablespoons olive oil

3 garlic cloves, minced

3 tablespoons white onions, minced

2 teaspoons salt

$1/4$ teaspoon pepper

***Put parsley into a food processor and process until very fine. Add beans, olive oil, garlic, onions, salt, and pepper, and process until smooth. Cover and refrigerate at least 1 hour before serving.

Fuzzy Bats

With a few scraps of felt, faux fur, and shiny beads or buttons, you'll have a cute fuzzy bat in no time!

by KELLIE LISKEY

- chalk pencil
- faux fur, any color
- felt
- scissors
- pins
- sewing machine or needle and thread
- 2 safety eyes (if intended for kids under 3) or 2 (10-millimeter) beads or buttons
- stuffing

1. Use a chalk pencil to trace patterns (pages 35 and 36) onto reverse of faux fur and felt. Make sure nap of fur goes in same direction on both sides. Cut out pieces. Cut wing and ear slits.

2. Use chalk pencil to draw wing design onto 2 felt wings. Pin wing layers together, with design on top.

3. With sewing machine or needle and thread, stitch wing layers together, following the design. Repeat with second wing.

4. Fold ear pieces in half and push one through each opening. Pin and sew in place.

5. Put wings into wing openings. Pin and sew in place.

6. Align body pieces and pin them together, fur-side in. Sew together, leaving about a 1/4-inch seam allowance. Pin and sew on bottom piece, leaving a 2-inch gap.

7. Turn bat right-side out by pulling wings through gap and gently flipping the rest through. (If using safety eyes, poke through fur and attach now instead of step 8.) Fill with stuffing. Stitch gap closed.

8. Attach beads or buttons for eyes.

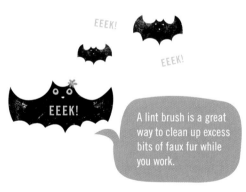

EEEK!

EEEK!

EEEK!

A lint brush is a great way to clean up excess bits of faux fur while you work.

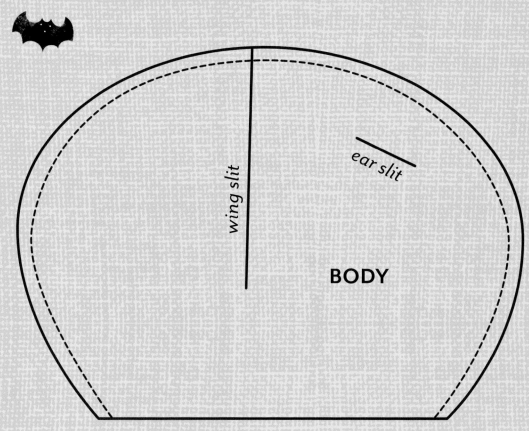

wing slit

ear slit

BODY

Cut 2 of this body pattern out of faux fur.
Then cut along wing and ear lines.

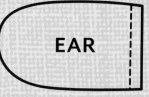

EAR

Cut 2 ears out of felt.

*Fuzzy bats are so quick and easy to make.
You'll finish before the stroke of midnight!*

——— — — —

cut   sew

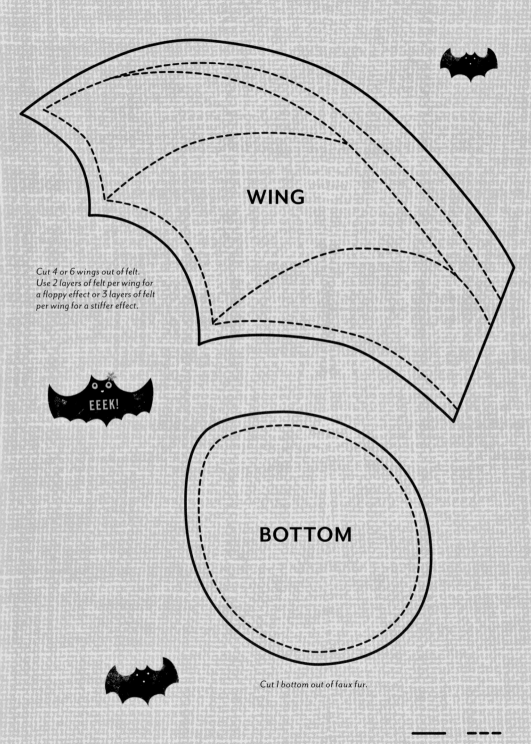

WING

Cut 4 or 6 wings out of felt.
Use 2 layers of felt per wing for
a floppy effect or 3 layers of felt
per wing for a stiffer effect.

EEEK!

BOTTOM

Cut 1 bottom out of faux fur.

cut   sew

Ghost Toasts

Add a dash of spookiness to soups and stews
with toasty ghost-shaped croutons.

by MAKI OGAWA

supplies

- white bread
- mini cookie cutters or knife
- straws in two different sizes
- butter

1. Cut ghosts and other fun shapes out of bread with cookie cutters or a knife.

2. Pinch one end of the wider straw to make an oval and then use it to punch out ghost mouths. Use the smaller straw to punch out eyes.

3. Over medium-low heat, warm butter in a pan and add bread ghosts; panfry until golden brown. Done!

You can trace these ghost and puffy cloud shapes or customize your own! Mini cookie cutters come in lots of spooky shapes, too.

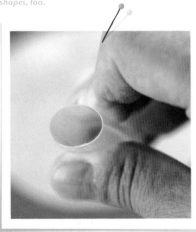

Pinch the end of a straw to make a tiny oval cutter.

Good Little Witch

This small-n-sweet sorceress can be made with any yarn you wish,
just choose a hook size that matches the yarn.

by SAYJAI T.

supplies

- C, D, or 3-millimeter hook
- 4-ply or worsted-weight yarn in the following colors: black, pink, cream, red
- stuffing
- red mohair yarn
- 1 (5-inch) square piece cardboard
- 2 (10-millimeter) black buttons or doll eyes

This project is working in continuous rounds; do not join or turn unless directed. Mark first stitch of each round.

EEEK!

FOOT AND LEG (MAKE 2): Round 1: With black yarn, ch 2; sc 6 in first ch {6}. **Round 2:** [Inc] around {12}. **Round 3:** [Sc 1, inc] around {18}. **Round 4:** [Inc, sc 2] around {24}. **Round 5:** Sc around in back loops only {24}. **Round 6:** Sc 10, [dec] 4 times, sc 6 {20}. **Round 7:** [Dec, sc 2] twice, [dec] 5 times, sc 2 {13}. Switch to pink. **Round 8:** Sc around in back loops only {13}. **Round 9:** Sc around {13}. **Round 10:** Sc around {13}. Switch to cream. **Round 11:** Sc around in back loops only {13}. **Rounds 12 and 13:** Sc around {13}. On first leg, sl in first sc. Fasten off. On second leg, don't sl in first sc and don't fasten off.

BODY AND HEAD: Round 1: With cream, hold legs together, with upper inner thighs together, and toes pointed forward. Insert hook in center of innermost spot of thigh of first leg, pull out loop from second leg, sc (do not count this st), sc 12 on second leg (mark first st), sc 12 on first leg {24}

Round 2: [Sc 2, inc] around {32}. Stuff legs. **Round 3:** Sc around {32}. Switch to black. **Round 4:** [Sc 7, inc] around {36}. **Round 5:** Sc around in back loops only {36}. **Rounds 6 to 9:** Sc around {36}. **Round 10:** [dec, sc 4] around {30}. **Round 11:** Sc 2, dec, [sc 3, dec] 5 times, sc {24}. **Round 12:** [Dec, sc 2] around {18}. Switch to cream. Stuff. **Round 13:** [Inc, sc 2] around in back loops only {24}. **Round 14:** Sc 5, inc 3 times, sc 9, inc 3 times, sc 4 {30}. **Round 15:** Sc 5, inc, [sc, inc] 2 times, sc 10, inc, [sc, inc] 2 times, sc 5 {36}. **Round 16:** Sc 6, inc, [sc 2, inc] 2 times, sc 11, inc, [sc 2, inc] 2 times, sc 5 {42}. **Round 17:** Sc 6, inc, [sc 3, inc] 2 times, sc 12, inc, [sc 3, inc] 2 times, sc 6 {48}. **Round 18:** Sc around {48}. **Round 19:** [Sc 7, inc] around {54}. **Round 20:** Sc around {54}. **Round 21:** [Sc 8, inc] around {60}. **Rounds 22 to 26:** Sc around {60}. **Round 27:** Sc 4, dec, [sc 8, dec] 5 times, sc 4 {54}. **Round 28:** Sc around {54}. **Round 29:** [Sc 7, dec] around {48}. **Round 30:** Sc around {48}. **Round 31:** Sc 3, dec, [sc 6, dec] 5 times, sc 3 {42}. **Round 32:** [Sc 5, dec] around {36}. **Round 33:** [Sc 4, dec] around {30}. **Round 34:** [Sc 3, dec] around {24}. **Round 35:** [Sc 2, dec] around {18}. Stuff. **Round 36:** [Sc, dec] around {12}. **Round 37:** [Dec] around, sl in first sc {6}. Fasten off.

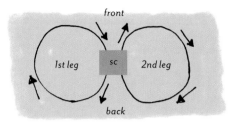

Attach legs to body like this in step 2.

3 SKIRT: **Round 1:** Using black, join in the front loops left from Round 4 with head pointed toward you. Sc around {36}. **Round 2:** Sc around {36}. **Round 3:** Sc around, sl in first sc {36}. Fasten off.

4 ARM (MAKE 2): **Round 1:** With black, ch 2, sc 6 in first ch {6}. **Round 2:** [Sc, inc] around {9}. **Rounds 3 to 7:** Sc around {9}. **Round 8:** Sc around {9}. Switch to cream. Stuff. **Round 9:** [Sc, dec] 3 times in back loops only {6}. **Round 10 (thumb):** Inc, skip next 4 sts, inc, sl first sc {4}. Fasten off. **Round 10 (hand):** With cream, join in the next free st on Round 9, inc 4 times {8}. **Round 11:** Sc around {8}. **Round 12:** Flatten last row, matching sts and working through both thicknesses, sc 2, sl st. Fasten off.

5 EDGE OF SLEEVES: Using black, join in the front loops left from Round 8 with top of arm pointed toward you. [Sc 2, inc] 3 times, sl in first sc. Fasten off {12}. Sew arms to body with thumbs toward front.

6 WITCH HAT: **Round 1:** With black, ch 2, sc 6 in first chain {6}. **Round 2:** Sc around {6}. **Round 3:** [Sc, inc] around {9}. **Round 4:** Sc around {9}. **Round 5:** [Inc, sc 2] around {12}. **Rounds 6 and 7:** Sc around {12}. **Round 8:** [Inc, sc 3] around {15}. **Round 9:** Sc around {15}. **Round 10:** [Sc 4, inc] around {18}. **Round 11:** Sc around {18}. **Round 12:** [Sc 5, inc] around {21}.

Round 13: Sc around {21}. **Round 14:** [Sc 6, inc] around {24}. **Round 15:** Sc around {24}. **Round 16:** [Inc, sc 7] around {27}. **Round 17:** Sc around {27}. **Round 18:** [Sc 8, inc] around {30}. **Round 19:** Sc around {30}. **Round 20:** [Sc 9, inc] around {33}. **Round 21:** Sc around {33}. **Round 22:** [Sc 10, inc] around {36}. **Round 23:** Sc around {36}. **Round 24:** [Sc 11, inc] around {39}. **Round 25:** Sc around {39}. **Round 26:** [Sc 12, inc] around {42}. **Round 27:** [Inc, sc 13] around {45}. **Round 28:** [Sc 14, inc] around {48}. **Round 29:** [Sc 15, inc] around {51}. **Round 30:** [Sc 16, inc] around {54}. **Round 31:** [Inc, sc 17] around {57}. **Round 32:** [Sc 18, inc] around {60}. **Round 33:** [Sc 9, inc] around {66}. **Rounds 34 to 35:** Sc around {66}. **Round 36 (brim):** [Sc, inc] around in front loops only {99}. **Rounds 37 to 39:** Sc around. {99} **Round 40:** Sc around, sl in first sc. Fasten off {99}.

7 HAIR AND FACE: Wind mohair yarn loosely and evenly around cardboard to cover; cut across one edge of cardboard. **For fringe:** Fold one strand of yarn in half. Insert hook in free loop of Round 35, draw folded end through stitch and pull loose ends through folded end; draw knot up tightly. Continue with the rest of the strands. Sew hat onto head. Style hair in pigtails or braids. Sew eyes 8 sts apart over Rounds 22 and 23 of head. Stitch on a smile with red thread.

To crochet a tiny jack-o-lantern for your little witch, download the free pattern: Irreference.com/Witch-Craft!

Halloween Cupcake Toppers

Happy Halloween! Print or trace these letters and designs
to customize treats for your friends and family.

by SARAH GOLDSCHADT

supplies

- an inkjet printer or tracing paper and pencil
- 2 sheets white card stock
- scissors and/or 1¼-inch circle punches
- double-sided tape or glue
- toothpicks
- 15 cupcakes or more

1. Copy and print or trace letters or designs.

2. Cut out all circles with scissors, or use a handy 1¼-inch circle punch.

3. Place a cutout facedown. Put a piece of double-sided tape in the middle; center a toothpick on top.

4. Place a matching cut-out on top, faceup, making sure the designs are aligned. Press firmly on both sides. The toothpick will create a slight ridge on the top cutout, but the side facing down will be flat and smooth.

5. Decorate with markers or glitter, if desired. Stick into cupcakes and have a party!

H A P P
Y H A L
L O W E
E N
!

Color copy these patterns or download the free PDF from Irreference.com/Witch-Craft.

Knitted Spider & Spiderweb Hat

This plush knitted spider can be sewn onto a fancy lace-knit cobwebby topper or stitched onto other caps or scarves.

by KATE OATES

supplies

- I skein white yarn and I skein black yarn, such as Berroco Comfort in pearl and liquorice
- US 7 (4½ millimeter) 16-inch circular needles
- set of five US 7 double-pointed needles
- stitch marker
- stuffing

KNITTED SPIDER

These patterns include sizing for 17½-inch infant (19-inch toddler or child, 21-inch adult small, and 23-inch adult large). Sizing is written for a loose fit; if you prefer a snug hat, size down for the cast-on but maintain length as written.

1 SPIDER'S BODY: With black yarn and double-pointed needles (DPNs), CO 6 sts (all sizes). Divide sts evenly over 3 needles, place marker and join in the round, being careful not to twist stitches. **Round 1:** Kf&b around {12}. **Round 2:** K1, Kf&b twice, K1 on needles 1 & 2, K4 on needle 3 {16}. *For infant size:* **Rounds 3 to 7:** K all sts, then skip to Round 11. *For other sizes:* **Rounds 3 to 10:** K all sts. **Round 11:** K1, skp, K2tog, K1 on needles 1 & 2, K4 on needle 3 {12}. **Round 12:** Skp, K2tog on each needle {6}.

Cut yarn and weave through remaining sts and secure, leaving a long tail for sewing. Fill with stuffing.

2 SPIDER'S HEAD: With black yarn and DPNs, CO 4 sts (all sizes). Divide sts as evenly as possible over 3 needles, place marker and join in the round, being careful not to twist stitches. **Round 1:** Kf&b around {8}. **Rounds 2 to 4:** K all sts {8}. **Round 5:** *Skp, K2tog; repeat from * around {4}. Cut yarn and weave through remaining st and secure, leaving a long tail for sewing.

3 SPIDER'S LEGS (4 SHORT AND 4 LONG): *For infant size:* Subtract ½ inch from length of each leg. *All other sizes:* Knit as written. *Long front and back legs:* CO 3 sts, work in i-cord for 4 inches. To make i-cord, knit the first row. Slide the stitches to the opposite end of the needle. With the working yarn at the bottom of the row, knit across again, pulling the working yarn up the back so you can work with it. *Short middle legs:* CO 3 sts, work in i-cord for 2½ inches.

(4) With white and circular needle, CO 110 (121, 132, 143) sts. Place marker and join in the round, being careful not to twist stitches. **Round 1:** *K1, sl 1 back to LH needle; with RH needle, lift next 8 sts 1 at a time over this st and off the needle, K the first st again, yo twice, K2; repeat from * around. 50(55, 60, 65) sts. **Round 2:** *K1, drop 1st yo, in 2nd yo, Kf&b twice, then K in the front of the st once more (5 sts in 1), K2; repeat from* around. 80(88, 96, 104) sts.

(5) Begin lace pattern (st count remains the same at the end of each round). **Round 3:** *K1, yo, K2tog, yo, K3tog, yo, K2tog, yo; repeat from * around. **Round 4:** *Yo, K1, yo, K2tog, yo, K3tog, yo, K2tog; repeat from * around. **Round 5:** *K2tog, yo, K1, yo, K2tog, yo, K3tog, yo; repeat from * around. **Round 6:** *Yo, K2tog, yo, K1, yo, K2tog, yo, K3tog; repeat from * around. **Round 7:** *K3tog, yo, K2tog, yo, K1, yo, K2tog, yo; repeat from * around. **Round 8:** *Yo, K3tog, yo, K2tog, yo, K1, yo, K2tog; repeat from * around. **Round 9:** *K2tog, yo, K3tog, yo, K2tog, yo, K1, yo; repeat from * around. **Round 10:** *Yo, K2tog, yo, K3tog, yo, K2tog, yo, K1; repeat from * around. Repeat rounds 3 to 10 until hat measures about 5½ (6½, 7½, 8½) inches from the brim, ending with an even-numbered round.

(6) For crown shaping, change to DPNs when needed. **Round 1:** *K2tog, yo, K3tog, yo, K2tog, yo, K1; repeat from * around. 70(77, 84, 91) sts. **Round 2:** *K2tog, yo, K3tog, yo, K2tog, yo; repeat from * around. 60(66, 72, 78) sts. **Round 3:** *K2tog, yo, K2tog, yo, K2tog; repeat from * around. 50(55, 60, 65) sts. **Round 4:** *K3tog, yo, K2tog, yo; repeat from *

around. 40(44, 48, 52) sts. **Round 5:** *K2tog, yo, K2tog; repeat from * around. 30(33, 36, 39) sts. **Round 6:** *K3tog, yo; repeat from * around. 20(22, 24, 26) sts. **Round 7:** *K2tog; repeat from * around. 10(11, 12, 13) sts. Cut yarn and weave through remaining sts and secure, weaving in yarn tail.

ASSEMBLY

(7) Sew tail from spider body onto hat. Sew on legs one by one: Connect 2 long front legs to the spider body where the spider head will go. Sew on four short legs in the middle (2 on each side) and then add 2 long back legs. Once all legs are secured, place the head on top (it will help hide where all the legs come together). Cut and weave in loose ends.

Creepy-crawly knitted spiders can be sewn onto anything imaginable—or tucked into cupboards or coat pockets for a scary surprise!

Lovely Wicked Tutus

Stitch up a fiendishly chic skirt in just a few hours,
and you'll be the belle of the midnight ball!

by JINX

supplies

- at least ½ yard lace
- scissors
- sewing machine or needle and thread
- at least 18 yards 54-inch-wide tulle
- elastic or stretch lace for waistband

1. Cut lace into 4 large, even squares. The easiest way is to remove the selvage and line up the two formerly selvaged ends. Fold back over to the cut ends, making a square. Cut into 4 pieces.

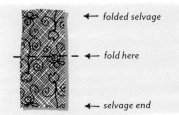

← folded selvage

← fold here

← selvage end

2. Fold each square in half, then in half again. Cut a partial circle out of the folded corner. The cut should be about $2^{1}/_{2}$ inches deep for an average adult, smaller for a child, and larger for a plus size.

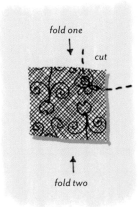

fold one
cut
fold two

3. Unfold fabric, and you'll have a hole in the center of each square. From the middle of one of the sides, cut to the hole. Repeat for all squares.

cut

4. Sew pieces together along cuts, making one long piece, with centers joining to make 1 long curved waistline at top and corners of all squares falling to the bottom.

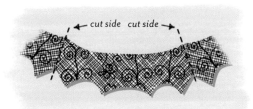

← cut side   cut side →

5 With sewing machine's gathering foot or a needle and thread, gather the entire length.

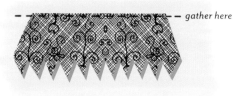

gather here

6 Lay gathered edge over waistband. Sew inside out so that the stitching will be on the underside of the fabric when finished.

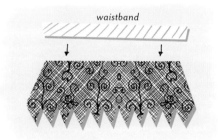

waistband

7 Add as many layers of tulle as you want, gathering and sewing each layer directly on top of the lace. Be as creative as you like with the length, fullness, and color. The possibilities are endless!

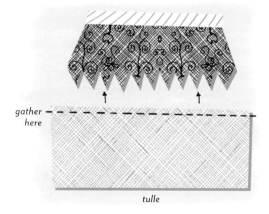

gather here

tulle

8 When finished layering, sew ends of waist band together, creating a circle.

Instead of perfectly ruffled lace, you can sew triangular fabric scraps into a quick and easy waistband.

Magical Catnapping Mask

With a satin-soft black-cat sleeping mask, you'll wake up
from a nap feeling like you've dozed a hundred years!

by NAOMI MATSUDA

supplies

- scissors
- chalk pencil
- 1 piece satin or other soft fabric
- 1 piece fleece
- 1 piece black elastic
- 1 piece tulle, cut to match ribbon
- 1 piece ribbon, about 2 inches long

1. Use a chalk pencil to trace patterns onto satin and fleece. Cut out pieces.

2. Place right sides of two back pieces together. With a $1/4$-inch seam allowance, sew for $1/2$ inch, leave a 2-inch gap, and continue sewing the last $1/2$ inch. Press seam open.

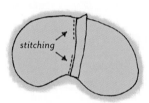

Leave a gap when you stitch the seam of your back satin piece.

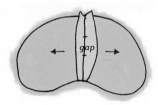

Press seam open. You'll turn mask right-side out through gap in step 4.

Sleeping-beauty bows are a dream to make out of any two pieces of ribbon, tulle, or lace. See step 5.

3. Cut a rectangle from center of fleece fabric, 2-inches long and $1/2$ inch from top and bottom, to match the gap in the back satin piece. Place front satin piece right side up and pin elastic ends to mask. Place back and front satin fabric right sides together, and place the fleece on top of the back piece.

4. Pull elastic through gap and pin in middle of fabric so that it won't catch when you sew around edge of mask. Pin all 3 layers together. Sew around edge, with a $1/4$-inch seam allowance. Turn right-side out through the gap, and then hand-stitch closed.

5. **For the bow:** Stitch down the middle of the tulle, pulling thread tightly to pucker fabric and create a bow. Repeat with ribbon. Attach tulle bow to ribbon bow with a few stitches and sew them onto mask under cat ear. Sweet dreams!

EEEK!

Cut 1 piece out of satin for front and 1 piece out of fleece for interior padding.

Cut 2 pieces out of satin for back.

Peanut Butter & Jelly Skull Sandwiches

Strawberry jam and a little pink and chocolate frosting turn
regular old PB&J into spooky skull sandwiches!

by MAKI OGAWA

supplies

- round white bread rolls or biscuits
- peanut butter
- strawberry jelly
- chocolate frosting
- pink strawberry frosting

1. Slice open bread rolls, cutting almost all the way through. Close rolls.

2. Use chocolate frosting to draw on skeleton teeth and eyes. Add dots of strawberry frosting for cheeks.

3. Once frosting has set and dried, gently spread peanut butter inside sandwiches. Spoon in lots of strawberry jelly, letting it gush out the sides. Serve as spooky snacks or party favors!

You can use condiment pencils to draw with homemade frosting! For where to find them, see page 93.

With colorful frostings, spreads, jams, and jellies, you can design your own sandwich monsters.

EEEK!

EEEK!

Plushie Poison Apples

Mirror, mirror, on the wall, who's the wickedest of them all?
With a little crafting magic, this sweet little plushie apple turns rotten to the core!

by JACKI GALLAGHER

* red, green, brown, white, and black felt or fleece
* needle and thread
* stuffing

1. Trace patterns onto felt and cut out (page 58). Stitch face onto one of the apple slices.

2. Stitch the outside seam of 2 apple pieces together. Repeat so that you have 2 sets of 3 pieces each. Line up the 2 sets so that the tops and bottoms match, as do the outsides.

3. Sandwich the stem and leaf so that they're inside the apple halves, with just a little bit poking out at top. Starting there, stitch around the edge, leaving about a $1/4$-inch seam allowance and a 1-inch gap at the bottom.

4. Turn the apple inside-out through the gap, and you'll have an apple body with a leaf and stem sticking out the top.

5. Fill with stuffing and then stitch the gap closed. If you're making a half-poisoned apple, cut a wavy circle out of black felt and stitch it onto the bottom of the apple by hand. Add extra black spots for a very bad little apple.

Use black felt for a truly rotten little fella.

It's easy to sew plushies with a machine or by hand. Stuff them with fiberfill, cotton batting, or fabric scraps.

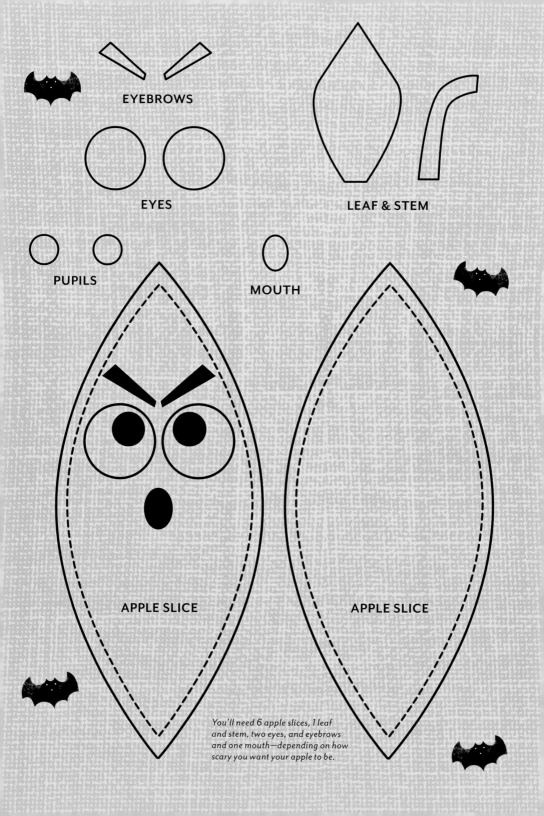

EYEBROWS

EYES

LEAF & STEM

PUPILS

MOUTH

APPLE SLICE

APPLE SLICE

You'll need 6 apple slices, 1 leaf and stem, two eyes, and eyebrows and one mouth—depending on how scary you want your apple to be.

Poison Ivy Lip Embellishment

This richly nourishing, restorative lip balm is an all-natural concoction. It contains no poison, only essential oils from herb leaves to create the flavor of dark, soft, green ivy.

by JILL MCKEEVER

supplies

- saucepan and spoon
- glass liquid measuring cup
- 3 tablespoons olive oil or sweet almond oil
- 2 tablespoons cocoa butter or shea butter
- 2 tablespoons beeswax
- a few sprigs fresh herbs, such as basil or marjoram (optional)
- 8 drops liquid stevia extract or 1 tablespoon honey
- oil from 2 vitamin E capsules or 2 to 3 drops oakmoss absolute
- a few drops essential oils, such as basil, petitgrain, geranium, and marjoram
- 12 ¼-ounce or 3 1-ounce clean tin containers

1. Create a bain-marie by filling a saucepan three-fourths with water and placing measuring cup in the center. Bring to a boil.

2. Warm olive oil or sweet almond oil in the measuring cup.

3. Add cocoa butter or shea butter and beeswax. Let melt, then stir to combine. If desired, add fresh herbs: Let steep 5 minutes, then remove herbs. Stir mixture until smooth. Remove measuring cup from saucepan.

4. Stir in stevia extract or honey and vitamin E or oakmoss.

5. Add assorted essential oils for ivy flavor. **A good ivy blend:** 9 drops sweet basil, 5 drops petitgrain, 3 drops geranium, and 3 drops marjoram. Stir until smooth, and quickly pour into containers.

Olive oil will give your concoction a green tint.

Lip balm containers can be store bought or vintage. For where to find them, see page 93.

Ruby Slippers

Be a DIY Dorothy with a pair of glitter-embellished shoes.

by ALICIA KACHMAR

supplies

- newspaper
- shoes with a smooth surface
- plastic bags
- all-purpose spray-on adhesive
- about 1 ounce red glitter
- spray-on acrylic coating in gloss finish

1. Prepare work surface with newspaper and make sure you're in a well-ventillated area. Better yet, work outside.

2. Stuff each shoe with a plastic bag so that only the sections that will be coated with glitter are exposed.

3. Spray half of one shoe with all-purpose adhesive and quickly coat with glitter (pour straight from container or use a spoon to sprinkle).

4. Repeat on other half. Shake lightly to see if you missed any spots; respray and coat with more glitter if necessary. Repeat steps 3 and 4 with second shoe.

5. Let dry half an hour. Shake off excess glitter onto newspaper. (Collect and pour back into container if desired.)

6. One at a time, cover shoes with spray-on acrylic coating.

7. Let dry 30 minutes. Remove plastic bags and shake off any excess glitter.

Brand new or vintage, any shoe with a fairly smooth surface can be transformed into sparkly, bewitching footwear.

For a smooth jewel-like finish, try using superfine glitter, such as the Martha Stewart Fine Glitter Set. For where to find it, see page 93.

Sleepy Ghost Brooches

With felt, thread, and a bit of stuffing, you can whip up
a pillowy little plush pal before naptime. *Zzz...*

by LINDSAY GIBSON

supplies

- chalk pencil
- small piece black felt, such as acrylic, wool, or eco-felt
- clasp pin or safety pin
- white embroidery thread and needle
- stuffing

1. Trace pattern (right) and cut ghost shapes from felt. Place pin in the middle of the back. Using white embroidery thread and a needle, sew it on with a few quick stitches until it feels nice and snug. Knot thread and set aside.

2. **For your ghost's face:** Use roughly 10 to 14 stitches for the eyes, 3 to 4 for the mouth, and 2 to 3 for the nose. It's up to you! Knot thread and cut off excess.

3. Align the two pieces, right sides facing out, and sew together starting at tail. Try a stitch size of about 3 millimeters with a little space between each stitch. Leave a 3/4-inch gap.

4. Keeping your needle and thread in place, fill your ghost with stuffing.

5. Stitch up the gap and knot thread on the backside of your new sleepy ghost pal. Happy napping!

You can stitch a little white ghost out of white felt and black or silver thread. Try adding sequins or googly eyes.

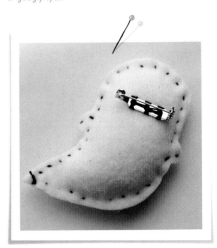

The back should look like this.

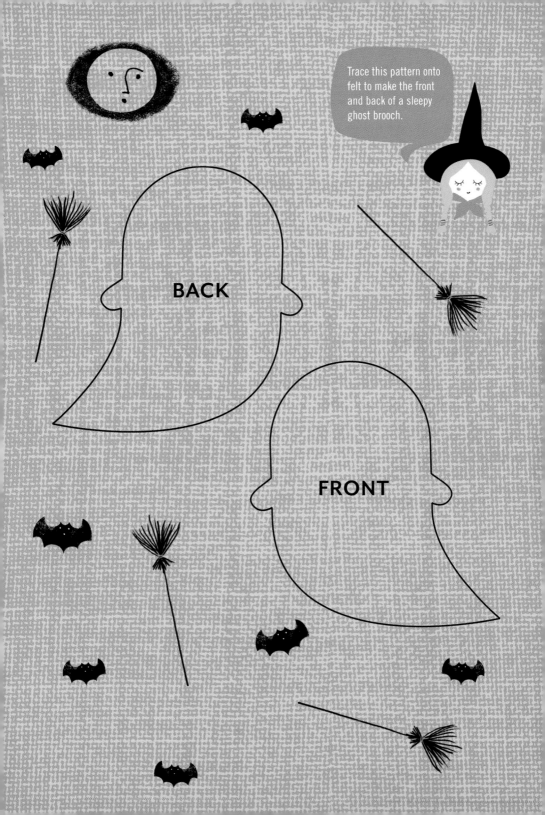

Trace this pattern onto felt to make the front and back of a sleepy ghost brooch.

BACK

FRONT

Spider Earrings

Stack glass beads onto wire and gently twist with
needle-nose pliers to create spooktacular spider earrings.

by ALEKSANDRA SASHA GIFFORD

- 2 metal eye pins (1 per spider)
- 2 (9-millimeter) black glass or acrylic beads (1 per spider)
- 2 (13-millimeter black and purple) lampwork glass polka dot beads (1 per spider)
- 2 (6- to 7-millimeter) black glass or acrylic beads (1 per spider)
- 20 (3- to 4-millimeter) white/seed beads (10 per spider)
- 4 (2-millimeter) green seed beads (2 per spider)
- needle-nose pliers
- 8 (6-inch) sections 24-gauge beading wire (4 per spider)
- 64 black glass bugle beads (32 per spider, 4 per leg)
- 50 (2-millimeter) purple seed beads (24 per spider)
- 2 (¼-inch) black chenille stems (1 per spider)
- 2 sections lightweight chain (1 per spider)
- 2 hook earrings (1 per spider)

1. **For each ghastly little fella's body:**
   Stack beads onto an eye pin: Slide on 1 (9-millimeter) black bead, 1 (13-millimeter) lampwork glass bead, and 1 (6- to 7-millimeter) black bead. To create the eyes and fangs, add 1 (3- to 4-millimeter) white seed bead, 2 (2-millimeter) green seed beads, and one more white seed bead.

2. With needle-nose pliers, pull excess wire snugly and coil it between first white seed bead and smaller black bead. Push the 2 white seed beads to the back, creating the fang effect! Repeat with second spider's body.

These beads work well, but you can use any types you like; just adjust the length of wire to fit. For great beading supplies, see page 93.

3 **For each creepy crawly's appendages:** With your hands, hold 4 sections of beading wire at once and bend up and down together. Fold them in half, joining the tips together. Place each spider's body in the middle, and wrap each half of the wire twice between lampwork glass bead and (6- to 7-millimeter) black glass bead.

4 While holding the body, use pliers to pull each wire taught, preparing it for beading. Adjust wires so they extend from body like legs.

5 **To bead each leg:** Slide on 1 black bugle bead followed by 1 purple seed bead, and repeat 3 more times, ending with a white seed bead. Coil excess wire tightly at end. Repeat. Bend legs into posture.

6 **Here's the secret special touch:** Wrap a black chenille stem around each spider's body. It covers wire leg joints with fuzz and completes flashy little spiders to cast that certain spell!

7 **For spider earrings:** Open up the last link in each chain with pliers. Loop it into eye pin and pinch closed. Repeat to affix hook earrings on opposite ends of chain.

From the wire loop at the end of each spider leg, you can tie ribbon or thread to make your arachnid into an ornament—or even add on extra beads and charms!

EEEK!

EEEK!

EEEK!

Tangerine Jack-o'-Lanterns

Oranges and tangerines are fun and easy to make
into miniature jack-o'-lanterns—great for lunchbox
treats, healthy snacks, and party favors!

by MAKI OGAWA

supplies

- toothpick
- knife
- citrus fruit, such as tangerines, oranges, or blood oranges
- lemon juice (optional)

1. With a toothpick, poke the dotted lines of a jack-o'-lantern face onto a tangerine.

2. Using a knife, cut through the peel (but not into the fruit flesh) along your dotted lines.

3. Slip knife under the peel at an angle to remove pieces.

4. Serve immediately or brush exposed fruit flesh with lemon juice to preserve freshness and color up to five hours.

You can carve faces onto all kinds of citrus fruits to make happy and healthy snacks.

Trick-or-Treat Garlands

With black and orange paper and a few yards of ribbon or yarn,
you can string up boo-tiful bunting before the clock strikes midnight!

by SARAH GOLDSCHADT

supplies

- 4 sheets orange and black card stock or thick paper
- tracing paper and pencil
- scissors or 2½-inch circle punch
- permanent marker, paint, or glitter
- tapestry needle and at least 3 yards orange yarn

1. Trace and cut 5 circles out of each color card stock, or use a handy circle punch. Trace witch hat and pumpkin patterns and cut out 10 from each color card stock.

2. With markers, glitter, or paint, draw on jack-o'-lantern faces and other decorations.

3. Glue witch hats to both sides of orange circles. Glue pumpkins to both sides of black circles.

4. Thread needle with yarn. String it through each circle and secure each one with a double knot. Alternate colors and space them 10 inches apart.

Trace witch hat and pumpkin patterns onto colored paper for garlands.

BOO!

EEEK!

EEEK!

Vampire Bite Necklaces

Create the illusion of Dracula's kiss with nothing
but a little yarn and your crochet hook!

by SANDY MEEKS

supplies

- C hook (2¾ millimeters)
- thread or yarn in a color that blends into your skin tone
- yarn in deep red and bright red
- tapestry needle and thread or gel super glue

1 **For necklace: Round 1:** Ch 2; 6 sc into 2nd chain from hook. **Round 2:** [Inc] around {12}. Sl st into next stitch and do not cut thread to make a toggle for clasp.

2 **Round 3:** Ch 80 to 90 stitches, depending on neck circumference. **Round 4:** Ch 10 and sc into the 10th ch from hook to make a loop. Sl st into the next 5 chains for a base to weave in end thread. Fasten off and weave in ends.

3 **For bite marks (make 2):** Use deep red yarn. **Round 1:** Ch 2; 6 sc into 2nd chain from hook. Sl st into next sc, making a small circle. Fasten off.

4 **First blood droplet with bright red yarn:** Ch 7; 3 sc into 2nd chain from hook, sl st into next 5 ch. Fasten off. **Second blood droplet with bright red yarn:** Ch 5, 3 sc into 2nd chain from hook, sl st into next 3 ch. Fasten off.

5 Sew bite marks onto droplets (or glue them together). Attach to necklace, about 1½ inches apart.

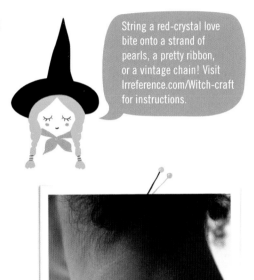

String a red-crystal love bite onto a strand of pearls, a pretty ribbon, or a vintage chain! Visit Irreference.com/Witch-craft for instructions.

Crochet a pretty toggle clasp in step 1.

Wicked Mary-Janes

With felt, ribbon, and beads or buttons, you can transform ordinary cotton shoes into zombie kittens, black cats, Dracula vs. Frankenstein, and more!

by LINDSAY GIBSON

supplies

- 1 pair cotton shoes, such as Mary-Janes, slippers, or slip-on canvas sneakers
- scissors
- sewing machine or needle and black thread
- 1 piece each pink, black, and white stiff ("friendly") felt
- heavy-duty plastic-friendly glue, such as E6000 craft adhesive
- 4 (18-millimeter) plastic cat eyes
- 2 (12-millimeter) pink plastic cat noses

1. Stuff shoes' toes with tissue paper for a tight, smooth work surface.

2. **For zombie kittens:** Trace and cut out 4 pink and 4 black felt triangles for ears. Center 1 pink triangle on top of 1 black triangle. With sewing machine set to zig-zag stitch, sew triangles together by going back and forth in a random pattern. Hand-stitching or machine-sewing with a straight stitch works too, but a zig-zag stitch creates an extra-rugged effect. Repeat with other pair. Trim loose threads.

3. Affix ears to shoes with a strip of glue along the bottom backs of ears.

4. From white felt, cut out 4 oblong shapes about 1½-inches long by ¼-inch wide. Place one on top of another in an X shape, and sew a black line down the middle with a sewing machine or by hand. Repeat. Trim loose threads.

5. With a strip of glue on back of each X shape, affix one to each shoe. Hold in place with fingertips until glue dries (a few minutes), pressing the felt flat to conform to the shape of the rounded shoe. Attach

plastic eyes to inner side of each shoe and affix noses in center of each shoe, or sew on button eyes and noses. Wait 24 hours before wearing.

To make cute black cats, use four eye beads, omit zigzag stitching, and decorate with ribbon bows.

See page 93 for where to find special cat beads; you can use pliers to remove screws from their backs, and then gently wipe clean for a smooth surface that can be glued to shoes. Googly eyes, pompoms, and buttons also make cute cat eyes and noses.

EEEK!

Trace these patterns onto felt to make Dracula vs. Frankenstein Mary-Janes, or design your own! Sew on facial features like Dracula's fangs and Frank's stitches with embroidery thread. Use (8- or 9-millimeter) round black plastic eyes, washed and with backs removed, or buttons.

EEEK!

DRACULA'S HAIR
(black)

DRACULA
(white)

DRACULA'S HEAD
(white)

DRACULA'S CAPE
(black)

FRANKENSTEIN'S BOLTS
(black)

FRANKENSTEIN
(white)

FRANKENSTEIN'S HEAD
(green)

FRANKENSTEIN'S HAIR
(black)

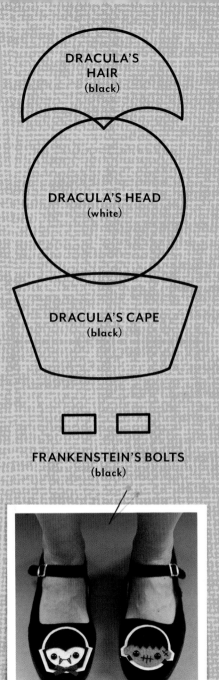

To make bows: *Tie short pieces of ribbon into bows. Cut off excess ribbon and seal the ends with clear nail polish or sealant to prevent fraying. Apply glue to center of bow and affix to shoes, decorating kitty ears or giving Dracula a handsome bowtie.*

Witches' Brew

Blood-orange punch served up in a fancy bowl
or creepy cauldron will keep guests under your spell.

by ALICIA KACHMAR

- 2 quarts cranberry juice or cranberry cocktail
- 1¾ quarts orange juice
- ¼ cup lemon juice
- 2 blood oranges, washed and sliced into ¼-inch-thick rounds
- 2 liters orange-flavored or unflavored seltzer

1. In a clean punch bowl or cauldron, stir to combine cranberry juice, orange juice, and lemon juice.

2. Add orange slices to the brew.

3. Pour in seltzer just before party time to ensure that witches' brew stays bubbly and fizzy for your guests.

For a potent punch, mix in 4 cups gin or vodka. Alternatively, spike your brew with 2 cups vodka plus 2 cups of orange liqueur, such as Cointreau.

Double, double, toil and trouble! A spiked witches' brew will turn any get-together into a wicked good time.

About the
Witch Crafters

From British Columbia to Japan to Southern California, these creative crafters make the magic happen.

Please visit our Web sites and online shops to say Hello!

SHALET ABRAHAM

Peculiar Momma
Peculiarmomma.blogspot.com
Bend, Oregon

Crystal Balls, Spell Jars & Homemade Snow Globes, page 24

There is a macabre side to my personality that is rarely seen. So I *love* Halloween because I can express my darker side all in the name of fun. Last fall I baked the most awesome witch's finger breadsticks and spider deviled eggs. Oh, but this year—this year there will be tons of eyeballs! At no other time of the year are these gruesome things socially acceptable. Same with ghost stories. In the daytime I'll tell you I absolutely do not believe in them. Ghosts? *Pfffth!* But at night, when it's dark and I'm all alone and the tree branches are rattling against the window—then I'm not so sure. You could very well find me trembling under the bed. As a child, shortly after my Grandfather's death, I had a very realistic dream where he appeared at the foot of my bed. I've never been quite able to shake the feeling that maybe it was real.

At any given time the kitchen table contains a sewing machine, my camera, yarn and knitting implements, jars of various sizes, tubes of paint, buttons, and an embroidery hoop or two. I typically work in the middle of mayhem as my children skirt around me—which means we all end up eating on the couch with our plates balanced on our knees.

Occasionally I sell my items on Etsy, but typically I craft for family and friends. I don't play favorites when it comes to crafting materials and methods: I dabble in whatever medium catches my fancy on any given day. I dream of having a studio, but in real life, I commandeer the kitchen table for my crafts.

FLOSSIE AREND

Knitting with Floss
Knittingwithfloss.blogspot.com
Astoria, New York

Dracula's Candy Bowl, page 28

I love everything about Halloween: bats, everything black, and the smell of the season, the sweet caramel scent of wood burning in crisp, cold air.

I started knitting recently and haven't needed or wanted anything else. I love my Denise interchangeable knitting needles. I just bought a Knit Kit, a measuring tape, stitch markers, scissors, row counter, and crochet hook all in one pocket-sized kit. It's indispensable. I tend to knit after work and on the weekends, often late into the night. I've spent entire Saturdays knitting and watching movie after movie.

I find a lot of inspiration on Ravelry.com, which is an online knitting and crocheting community. Fashion from the 1940s is a big interest of mine as well. I really enjoy what Wenlan Chia is doing with bulky, origami-style knits—things that can be folded or turned inside out and worn a different way. I love everything that Susan Crawford is doing at Knitonthenet.com, and her book *A Stitch in Time* is a wonderful example of beautifully executed vintage knits. I would be remiss if I didn't say I loved Roald Dahl as a creator of story and fantasy. Reading his works has made me a more creative person and helped develop my imagination.

"The real secret of magic is that the world is made of words, and if you know the words that the world is made of, you can make of it whatever you wish."

—TERENCE MCKENNA

JACKI GALLAGHER
Plush Off
Plushoff.com
Kamloops, British Columbia, Canada

Poison Apples, page 56

Homemade crafts are the perfect thing to do alone, with family, or with friends on a cool crisp fall day. I really enjoy working with felt: It's so pliable and it comes in so many wonderful colors that I'm continually inspired to make new crafts.

I'm not a night owl—I am very much a day creeper. I have a three-year-old autistic son who thinks I should wake up every morning, and so I do. Thankfully he loves sleep too, and rarely wakes before nine AM. We play, and

read, and cut and sew throughout the day. He inspires me daily!

If my son wakes up and asks to make an apple tree, well, that's what we do. If my friends are looking high and low for obscure pink things, I make a piece of pink toast. It's all in creativity and a whole lot of love for whimsy. Mealtimes are a big inspiration to me, as is the grocery store. I always have a notepad with me so I can jot down ideas wherever I am.

I don't really remember a lot of my Halloween costumes from childhood, but now that I have a child, I love that I can make my son his costume. This year he wanted to be Swiper from *Dora the Explorer*, but they don't make or sell Swiper costumes. So I made him one, and he loved it!

"It takes a lot of courage to show your dreams to someone else."

—ERMA BOMBECK

LINDSAY GIBSON
Em & Sprout
Emandsprout.etsy.com
Emandspout.blogspot.com
Southern California

Sleepy Ghost Brooches, page 63

Wicked Mary-Janes, page 75

I love all animals, but cat themes are a major part of Em & Sprout. (My brand is named after my two cats, after all). I'm inspired by cuteness, whimsy, and little things in life, like cloud-watching and preparing delicious meals.

My favorite crafting methods are sewing, screen-printing, and appliqué. I adore felt for its versatility, especially friendly felt! You can do so much with it, plus it's affordable (always a bonus). I also love using ribbon, pretty embroidery thread, and cute fabric. I can spend hours in craft stores just playing with the materials. It's an addiction!

My favorite creative people are the ones who are in touch with their inner child. If I have to pick one artist who sticks out in my mind, it would be Yoshitomo Nara, a contemporary Japanese pop artist. As for witchy types, I like Hermione Granger. And I always liked Sam from *Bewitched*, but mostly because I was jealous of her adorable nose wiggle.

I enjoy ghost stories and scary movies, but in small doses. I get creeped out very easily, which is why I prefer to keep my ghosts and creepers of the night cute. I'll admit that Halloween is my favorite holiday, and as an adult I still dress up! When I was a child, my little brothers and I would get dressed up and go trick-or-treating, visit all the neighborhood homes, and then come home and swap candy. I miss trick-or-treating. My favorite childhood costume was the year I decided to forgo any girly costume and become the Wolfman! I love seeing the costumes and decorations people come up with every fall—but I especially love it when ordinary folks go out of their way to turn their humble abodes into awesome haunted houses for both friends and strangers to enjoy.

"In naptime we succeed!"
—LINDSAY GIBSON

ALEKSANDRA SASHA GIFFORD
Wild Pearly's Lucid Beads and Designs
Wildpearly.blogspot.com
Etsy.com/shop/WildPearly
Wildpearly.etsy.com
Myspace.com/changeyourbeads
Chicago, Illinois

Spider Earrings, page 66

I am always "drunk as a hoot owl" on creativity, so I can craft day and night until my designs are complete. I think that the power of creation is very important and the inspiration for it lies deep down in our roots and folklore, our myths and legends, our dreams and our subconscious. I find my inspiration in art history and history in general; I find it in nature, astronomy, myths, dreams, exotic places, urban-industrial landscapes, romantic Goth stories and images. I also find inspiration in special characters and in people who are lost in time, books, superstitions, alchemy and mysticsm, etc.

I'm a fan of fuzzy, colorful, antique, Victorian, Goth, edgy, funky, and bohemian styles—which gives me plenty of room for mixing materials and crafting methods and techniques. I create by impulse and pure intuition. For me there are no preparation sketches and measurements; everything comes out like a beautiful storm.

SARAH GOLDSCHADT*

*My name is pronounced "SAHR-ah," the Danish pronunciation
Sarahgoldschadt.com
Goldylocks.etsy.com
St. Paul, Minnesota & Copenhagen, Denmark

Trick-or-Treat Garlands, page 71

Halloween Cupcake Toppers, page 42

I'm a morning person and love working on bright, sunny days. I find inspiration in travel, thrift stores, dollar stores, patterns found in everyday life, and craft blogs. I like anything Scandinavian in design: very simple, graphic, and lots of white! I love to design on my computer, take pictures, sew, knit, crochet, and make things out of paper.

My favorite creative people are Sandra Juto (Sandrajuto.com) and Elisabeth Dunker (Finelittleday.blogspot.com). When I was a child, my mother made me a princess costume out of white fabric with glitter glued into swags along the bottom. The dress was reused again when we dyed it blue and added an apron to make me Dorothy from *The Wizard of Oz*. The Wicked Witch of the East had a great style, with striped black and white stockings and ruby red slippers.

Ghost Busters is about the only ghost-related movie that I enjoy. But I love carving pumpkins and hosting pumpkin-carving parties. I also enjoy the cheesy Halloween decorations you can find in dollar stores. The plastic spiders and creepy crawlies are so fun!

"Twenty years from now you will be more disappointed by the things that you didn't do than by the ones you did do. So throw off the bowlines. Sail away from the safe harbor. Catch the trade winds in your sails. Explore. Dream. Discover."

—MARK TWAIN

GRACE HIURA

CakeLab
Cakelabnyc.com/blog
Cakelab.etsy.com
New York, New York

Cupcake Graveyard, page 26

I love to bake, and I also enjoy making handmade greeting cards and miniature food jewelry. (I'm a wee bit food obsessed.) I don't really craft on a schedule, but it does always end up being late at night. I love the quiet and peace of the city night. And inspiration is everywhere—a color, a smell, a childhood memory. I love crisp autumn evenings, the smell of the leaves, caramel apples, orange-y new moons, and cozy sweaters. My baking is inspired by childhood treats, from my old favorites to foods I wasn't allowed to eat. I actually never had a s'more until I was an adult!

My two favorite creative people are Sable Yong (Etsy seller, Sabletoothtiger) and Simone Jung. Sable screen prints all the witty, snarky things I wish I had thought to say, and Simone is a rose-colored-eyeglass-wearing writer trying to find her niche while making felty things and knitting scarves for her ten grandmothers. That or the two grandmothers who just really like scarves.

Although I don't remember my favorite Halloween costume as a child, I do remember my least favorite: My mother made matching bunny costumes for my younger brother and me, in pink and light blue. Ridiculous. We may have received extra sympathy candy from our neighbors. Thanks, Mom! I have always wanted a dress like Glinda the Good Witch's, and I have always admired the command that the Sea Hag wields over her "goons" in *Popeye*. That's pretty neat. I gotta look into getting me some goons.

"MINE" and "NOW" accompanied by a finger point usually expresses what I'm thinking most of the time.
—BOSSY BEAR

JINX
MTCoffinz
MTcoffinz.com
MTcoffinz.etsy.com
MTcoffinzUnderground.etsy.com
Stores.ebay.com/MTCoffinz
Shanalogic.com
Hartford, Connecticut

Lovely Wicked Tutus, page 48

My name is Jinx, but most people refer to me as the Coffee-Fueled Sewing Robot. As far as crafting goes, I think spontaneity is the best method. My best results come from noticing something and instantly knowing what it is going to become. Sometimes it takes a while for it to turn out just right, but I always know at first sight. In spite of my spontaneity, I have a daily routine. I wake up to Halloween every day with my real-life *Addams Family*, grind fresh coffee, check e-mail, and start sewing. Bedtime comes whenever I am too exhausted to see straight—usually around three AM!

I like Tim Burton, Marilyn Manson, and Morticia Addams, so it's no surprise that I'm a big fan of Halloween. I know spiders and bats are a little cliché, but I have loved that theme since I was a little kid.

On my desk, two stone gargoyles guard my craft secrets. I also have a giant picture above my table that looks like a Victorian couple, but when you look again it shifts into two horrible monsters. And I love a good ghost story. I actually believe in ghosts. We have a real one in our house. We can hear him walking up the stairs. He also rings the doorbell—which we don't even have, but we hear the chimes very clearly! *Spooky.*

ALICIA KACHMAR
Eternal Sunshine
Eternalsunshine.etsy.com
Aliciakachmar.com/blog
New York, New York

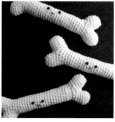

Creepy Crocheted Bones, page 19

Freaky Finger Food, page 31

Ruby Slippers, page 61

Witches' Brew, page 78

My birthday falls two days after Halloween (Day of the Dead!), so I have thrown lots of intricately planned Halloween-costume birthday parties. I grew up in western Pennsylvania where autumn meant beautiful leaves, apple cider, hiking in the woods, and cooling temperatures. Both my mom and dad are very good with their hands. I remember them denying my sister and me many times when we asked them to buy us something, but never denying us when we wanted to make something, to create something. No matter how busy they were or what time it was—whether we wanted to make salt dough or learn how to sew a purse—we were allowed to create it.

As an adult I don't always dress up for Halloween, but I attend the Halloween Extravaganza and Procession of Ghouls at the St. John the Divine cathedral: It pairs a silent black-and-white film with haunting, live organ music, followed by a procession of spookily costumed people courtesy of the amazingly talented designer, puppet-maker, and artist-in-residence Ralph Lee. I'm always thinking about how inanimate objects would feel, in the same way that children attach feelings to stuffed animals and the like. I used to be a teacher/nanny/daycare worker, so I was constantly exposed to and amazed at how children saw their surroundings in such a poetic and deep way.

Today, creating is my main business. My work is available in my Etsy shop and at a handful of New York City brick-and-mortar shops. I am primarily a crochet and knit designer, but I also dabble in paper craft, sewing, cross-stitch, and soap-making, and I'm always looking to learn something new. I love taking crochet or knitting on the subway in New York because it's a great way to pass the time if I can't focus on a novel, and sometimes conversation will ensue between a curious onlooker and myself.

"I will not reason and compare: my business is to create."

—WILLIAM BLAKE

CAROL LIN
SpecialMeat
Specialmeat.etsy.com
Facebook.com/specialmeat
Diamond Bar, California

KELLIE LISKEY
Zygopsyche
Kellieliskey.com
Zygopsyche.etsy.com
Salem, Oregon

Bottled Potions, page 13

Fuzzy Bats, page 33

Oftentimes, when it comes to crafting, one idea is the gateway to a whole slew of them. It is good to have people you can depend on for honest opinions and suggestions. My long-term boyfriend and my sister are like my counselors. I try to stay eco-friendly when selecting materials, and I love anything pretty and cute. I always have a small sketchbook and a pen handy in case I come up with new ideas or run across new information throughout the day. I get a lot of inspiration from other artists and fairy tales. Some of my favorite artists include Alphonse Mucha and Yulia Brodskaya. And I love the *Harry Potter* series; I'm very partial to Severus Snape.

I love the color of autumn leaves! Unfortunately, where I live in California, the leaves do not change color very much. My family always hands out candy on Halloween, even when all the kids in the neighborhood have grown up. I thought I grew out of the dress-up stage, but that may change soon. I try not to believe in ghost stories. I am such a big chicken. Spooky movies have always attracted me, but I'm too scared to watch them!

"Simplicity is the ultimate sophistication."
—LEONARDO DA VINCI

People in the crafting community know me as Zygopsyche, which is a word I made up a long time ago in college to mean a union of minds or souls. I believe art does that for people.

I am a soft sculpture and fabric loving girl at heart. So if it feels good, I'll make something out of it. I find much of my inspiration in nature; I love animals and being out in the garden. I am generally a morning person, but with a husband who loves staying up late, I find myself staying up past midnight many evenings. As for habits, routines, and schedules, they all went out the window a long time ago. I do, however, have daily goals I like to fulfill by bedtime.

Halloween is my favorite holiday—and my wedding anniversary! I love carving pumpkins, apple cider, and the changing leaves of fall. When I was young, my favorite dress-up costume was a gypsy fortune teller probably because I got to raid my mother's costume jewelry drawer and make up crazy fortunes for everyone. My favorite bewitching icon would have to be the Wicked Witch of the West from *The Wizard of Oz*. I drove my parents nuts cackling like her when I was little.

NAOMI MATSUDA

Naomilingerie.blogspot.com
Naomilingerie.etsy.com
Melbourne, Australia & Hiroshima, Japan

Magical Catnapping Mask, page 51

When I was growing up in Japan, there was a famous cartoon character named Sally the Witch, and I wanted to be a witch just like her! Although I've always liked fantasy stories like *The Lord of the Rings*, I don't like ghost stories; Japanese ones are particularly scary. (I think I believe in ghosts, so maybe that's why I'm afraid.) In Japan I don't celebrate Halloween, but sometimes I'll wear a costume for the occasion. Years ago, I made a Tinker Bell costume with my friends, and it would be fun to dress up like Cat Woman!

I love to travel, and I find inspiration in beautiful things—especially antiques, vintage fashion, and kimonos. I love film director Sofia Coppola's girlish style. My favorite materials are chiffon, organdy, satin, tulle, and lace. I have a part-time day job, so I do my sewing later in the day, typically from six to ten in the evening.

JILL MCKEEVER

For Strange Women
Forstrangewomen.com & Catvoices.com
Kansas City, Missouri

Poison Ivy Lip Embellishment, page 59

Halloween has always been by favorite holiday and perhaps the only one I ever feel like celebrating, besides equinoxes and solstices. My Catholic mother never let me dress up as anything scary as a child, which maybe led me to express my Gothic side as an adult instead!

My favorite materials are plant distillations and extractions and anything from nature. I love natural perfumery and scented products, jewelry making, package design, and anything with a strange twist. I find inspiration in the forest and all its intricacies, my animal friends, and music—as well as lost civilizations and loving cultures. Influences include Victorian design, packaging, and writing; forest patterns and colors; and anything antique.

Musicians inspire me. I love Stevie Nicks (who doesn't?), Siouxie Sioux, and Melora Creager. Many of my favorite musicians are also visual and conceptual artists as much as they are recording and performance artists. I love the idea of combining several art forms at one time.

For someone with dark and moody tendencies, I certainly like daylight, and someday wish to see more of it. I currently work every day from about nine in the morning until six to ten at night, but I do take tea breaks. I am hoping to figure out ways to cut my work time to 50 hours a week. Thankfully, I have a Russian blue familiar named Jaqk. And I love to watch dark comedies and strange, creepy movies, such as *Beetlejuice*, *Eraserhead*, *Lost Highway*, *The Shining*, *Sunset Boulevard*, and *Donnie Darko*. I also always loved the romance between Morticia and Gomez in the Addams Family. I can't help but like Maleficent, even though witchcraft should not really be used destructively.

"Animals like me though folks turn away,
 I like the pigeons, I like what they say."
— RASPUTINA

SANDY L. MEEKS
Meeks Sandy Girl
Meekssandygirl.etsy.com
Hot Springs, Arizona

Crochet Vampire Bite Necklace, page 73

For more than ten years, I've been recycling cashmere yarn from damaged sweaters that I get from a local department store. Needless to say, I love cashmere and have quite the stash in almost every color imaginable! Any kind of hook and any kind of yarn will do. Many mornings I wake up to inspiration and can't wait to get the coffee and the crochet hook going.

My father loves art and has visited some of the most famous museums around the world, so I grew up with his stories and pictures of his travels. And my mother can sew, quilt, embroider, crochet, macramé—I think she can do it all! She taught me how to embroider and sew when I was very young, and then she taught me how to crochet when I was twenty-five. I've been crocheting ever since. My husband Chris is the most amazing artist I have ever met. Once while we were playing Guitar Hero he suggested I make a scarf to match the scales in the game, and I made one to resemble a scale for a song that he loves. He shows it off to everyone. My son and I dress up for Halloween. Zombies are our favorite! When I was nineteen, I played a vampire in a haunted house. I did my own makeup, and I scared my young cousin who went running out of there as fast as his little eight-year-old legs could take him.

KATHRYN LINDSAY OATES
Tot Toppers (my children's line) &
When I Grow Up (my adult line)
MakeTotToppers.etsy.com
TotToppers.com
Lexington, South Carolina

Knitted Spider & Spiderweb Hat, page 45

I am a knitting night owl! But I also bring my needles with me wherever I go, should there be a spare moment to knit—which can be difficult to find, since I have two children and am finishing up a dissertation. I mostly cable and Fair Isle knit with yarn (yarn, and more yarn), but I have been known to crotchet an edge here and there. I also do lacework. Ask your local yarn store if they carry my patterns! You can also buy electronic copies of my patterns through my Web site, Knit Picks, Ravelry, Patternfish, Etsy, you name it.

I find inspiration mostly in my children. Sometimes outside. I like everything whimsical and funky—which is what I love most about Halloween and creepy-cute things. I remember one Halloween, I dressed up as a pregnant woman: I wore some of my mom's maternity clothes, put rollers in my hair, and drew varicose veins on my legs! And, like I said, I love a bit of whimsy. When I was a child, I loved *I Dream of Jeannie* and *Bewitched*. I have also been known to watch *The Vampire Diaries* on a regular basis, and, yes, I read the *Twilight* series!

MAKI OGAWA
Cute Obento
CuteObento.com
Flickr.com/photos/cuteobento
Saitama, Japan

Chocolate Marshmallow Skulls, page 17

Ghost Toasts, page 37

Peanut Butter & Jelly Skull Sandwiches, page 54

Tangerine Jack-o'-Lanterns, page 69

For myself and my boys, I like to design cute bento boxes (Japanese boxed lunches) filled with a rainbow of healthful foods that are shaped to look like characters from fairy tales or children's books, arranged in a pretty, decorative way.

Halloween isn't a major holiday in Japan, but many Japanese mothers make special Halloween-themed bento boxes for their children in autumn. Our family visited Hawaii in September, and we found fun Halloween costumes and treats at the supermarket. My youngest son wanted to buy lots of gummy worms and chocolate eyeballs! We wished we could stay in Hawaii for trick-or-treating.

Like most boys, my sons like spooky stories and creepy things. When they think of ghosts, they imagine *Casper* and *The Little Ghost* instead of traditional Japanese ghosts (which are much scarier) because they love to watch classic American cartoons and the Cartoon Network. So they really enjoy Marshmallow Skulls and Peanut Butter & Jelly Skull Sandwiches, and other creepy-cute snacks that we make together.

SAMANTHA PURDY

The Pin Pals
Thepinpals.typepad.com
Thepinpals.etsy.com
Montreal, Quebec, Canada

Cross-Stitch Witch & Friends, page 21

My partner Sara Guindon and I are the crafters behind The Pin Pals! My favorite materials are DMC embroidery floss, embroidery needles, Aida cloth, graph paper, vintage and scrap fabric, beads, and tapestry yarn. And my first love is cross-stitch, which I love so much because all of the stitches are in tiny, neat rows! But I am also a great fan of quilting and using scrap and vintage fabrics to create functional items like handbags and make-up cases.

Some of my favorite artists and crafters are Erica Wilson, Brian Wildsmith, Celestino Piatti, Robert-Émile Fortin, Mary Blair, and Jerome Snyder; but there are so many I'm missing! Thrift shopping is one of my biggest sources of inspiration, along with riding the bus and reading books and blogs. My grandma influenced me a lot; she was very crafty and spent a lot of time putting tiny decorations on Christmas gifts, embroidering sleeping bags, and the like. Both my mom and grandma have a way of bringing inanimate objects to life. I'm also influenced by children's book illustration, Japanese stationery, and miniatures.

Autumn is my favorite season for all the colors and imagery that come with Halloween is especially fun, and I love any night filled with make-believe, spooky stories, and ghosts! My mom loved the show *Bewitched* and I'm actually named Samantha because of it.

When I was thirteen, I was convinced that any day I would find out I was a witch, or at least that I had magical powers: I remember preparing myself for when it happened. I would think things like, "It will be hard to hide it from my family, but maybe once it happens, they'll know, and reveal to me that they've had magical powers all along!" So, naturally, I loved Halloween as a kid, and although I don't celebrate it as much anymore, walking along tree-lined streets at night and looking at glowing pumpkins is still a favorite fall activity.

RACHEL SAUVAGEOT

Rachel Sauvageot
Heart of Light
Heart-of-light.blogspot.com
Heartoflight.etsy.com
Los Angeles, California

Bewitching Headbands & Corsages, page 10

I'm a big morning person and I have my most productive hours in the morning, over a hot cup of tea (or three!). I'm inspired by funny little things: Textures, lush gardens, and beautiful fabric catch my eye and I'll play with them until I have a design. I have a huge admiration for vintage accessories from the 1930s and 1940s because I love that the women of that period favored sharp, often plain tailoring but dressed it up with fabulous brooches and hats. You don't need nearly as many clothes if you have great accent pieces. I frequently go fabric hunting with accessories in mind. Hand-stitching is my favorite sewing method because it's so calming and you can do it anywhere. I almost always listen to the radio while I work because it keeps my mind occupied without distracting me: I can listen to *This American Life* for hours on end. When I'm not sewing, I'm writing for my blog or reading hundreds of others, like Amy Karol of Angry Chicken and Sarah Neuburger of The Small Object.

Autumn is one of my favorite seasons because the air is crisp, the light is golden, and the feeling of change is everywhere. I love Halloween because it's a purely fun holiday and you can be anyone you want to be for the day. My sister and I were lucky because we grew up in Southern California where it's warm enough to wear whatever costume you like. The biggest hit in our household was the dinosaur costume which consisted of a little green stegosaurus cap and cape with cute little cloth spikes, worn with a green leotard and tights. Between the two of us, we wore that costume for six years straight! We also frequently dressed up as gypsies so we could have an excuse to raid our mother's closet and jewelry drawer. When it comes to witches, I've always had a soft spot for Jeannie in *I Dream of Jeannie* because she wasn't scary and didn't have warts—but she did have great clothes.

SAYJAI THAWORNSUPACHAROEN
Amigurumi Crochet Patterns by K & J Dolls
Kandjdolls.blogspot.com
Kandjdolls.etsy.com
Bangkok, Thailand

Good Little Witch, page 39

I love yarn, and I love to crochet whenever I get a chance—mostly while my kids are at school or sleeping. My children and their toys are some of my biggest crafting inspirations. I also find inspiration from holiday seasons and from browsing photos on the Internet, and I've been influenced by both Thai and Western crochet designers. My favorite crafters are Annie Potter and Carolyn Christmas.

In Thailand it's very hot most of the year (except for December—my favorite month), so we don't really have autumn. And, although we don't celebrate Halloween here, my kids saw a Halloween celebration once at an international school and got scared! They talked about it for weeks. But, generally, we only know Halloween from merchandise and movies. I enjoy spooky books and ghost movies, and I believe in some ghost stories. Many Thai believe in house spirits and good luck amulets to protect you.

"Never say "I can't!" before you try."
—SAYJAI

Dark Arts & Crafts

SHOPPING GUIDE

Most projects in this book can be crafted from everyday items you already have on hand or could find at your local arts and crafts store. These online vendors carry simple, essential tools and supplies as well as all sorts of strange and wonderful treats that make craft time extra special.

AMAZON (AMAZON.COM):
Third-party sellers have lots of crafty items for sale, and Amazon has an endless supply of beads and buttons, fabrics and yarns, and tools and accessories. Check out their Home & Garden section for Sewing, Craft, and Hobby.

B & J FABRICS (BANDJFABRICS.COM):
This family-owned fabric store says they provide "possibly the best fabrics in the world"—and they just might be right.

BAKE IT PRETTY (BAKEITPRETTY.COM):
This online shop stocks lovely baking products and accessories, everything from cookie cutters to cake shimmer (perfect for bottled potions and Halloween cakes and cupcakes). Visit their Halloween theme shop for creepy cupcake liners and edible decorations!

BELLA REGALO (ETSY.COM/SHOP/BELLAREGALO):
Bella Regalo sells small feathers that fit inside tiny bottles for bottled potions, as well as beautiful exotic feathers that can be sewn onto crafts like bewitching headbands & corsages.

BRANDYWINE JEWELRY SUPPLY (BRANDYWINEJEWELRYSUPPLY.COM):
Brandywine Jewelry Supply carries lead-free and tarnish-free jewelry wire, great for use in spider earrings, bottled potions, and more.

BROWN BETTY (BROWNBETTYDESSERTS.COM):
For cupcakes like the ones on page 26, place an order at Brown Betty or your local cupcake bakeshop.

CANDYLAND CRAFTS (CANDYLANDCRAFTS.COM):
Creative candy and cupcake supplies are fun for decorating Halloween cupcakes and skull sandwiches, and inventing your own tricky treats.

CHAOTIC SUPPLIES (ETSY.COM/SHOP/CHAOTICSUPPLIES):
This independent vendor offers small corked bottles for perfect bottled potions.

CHARMS GALORE (ETSY.COM/SHOP/CHARMSGALORE):
Charms Galore carries small corked bottles that are great for bottled potions, as well as lockets, buttons, beads, and other enchanting charms.

COVER BUTTONS (COVERBUTTONS.COM):
This vendor carries button covers perfect for creating cross-stitch witch & friends (page 21), as well as your own custom cross-stitch accessories.

CREATE FOR LESS (CREATEFORLESS.COM):
This online shop offers all sorts of fine craft supplies at affordable prices.

EBAY (EBAY.COM):

If you know what you're looking for, eBay is a great place to find creepy-cute craft supplies.

ETSY SHOPS (ETSY.COM):

Individual sellers provide an endless selection of wicked accessories, craft supplies, and tools—not to mention inspiration.

FROM JAPAN WITH LOVE (FROMJAPANWITHLOVE.COM):

This cute shop carries condiment drawing pencils as well as sandwich cutters and other fun supplies.

JO-ANN FABRICS (JOANN.COM):

Craft stores like Jo-Ann's offer a wonderful variety of everyday supplies as well as hard-to-find items, such as spray-on adhesive for ruby slippers or clasp pins for sleepy ghosts.

KITCHEN KRAFTS (KITCHENKRAFTS.COM):

Known as the "foodcrafter's supply catalog," Kitchen Krafts stocks home baking supplies perfect for making magical treats.

MAUYA (MAUYA.COM):

Mauya carries star paper you can use to make your own mini origami stars, plus cute Japanese toys, lunch boxes, and charms.

MICHAELS CRAFT STORES (MICHAELS.COM):

Craft stores like Michaels are great places to pick up affordable supplies like felts, yarns, and sewing necessities. Plus Martha Stewart superfine glitter perfect for DIY ruby slippers.

MOOD FABRICS (MOODFABRICS.COM):

Visit Mood for an amazing selection of affordable designer fabrics of all kinds.

MOUNTAIN ROSE HERBS (MOUNTAINROSEHERBS.COM):

Mountain Rose Herbs carries all the herbs and essential oils you'll need for poison ivy lip embellishment.

THE PARTY WORKS (THEPARTYWORKS.COM):

The Party Works sells a wide variety of cake shimmer (for bottled potions and fun Halloween cakes and cupcakes), plus a wide variety of fun party supplies for all occasions.

REPRODEPOT (REPROTDEPOT.COM):

We love Repro Depot's vintage reproduction and retro fabrics and Japanese-import fabrics, lovely buttons, ribbons, iron-on patches, patterns and special craft and sewing tools.

SKS BOTTLE & PACKAGING (SKS-BOTTLE.COM):

This vendor offers all sorts of metal tins and containers perfect for poison ivy lip embellishment and other tiny treats.

SOAP CRAFTERS (SOAPCRAFTERS.COM):

Soap Crafters carries a wide variety of handy crafting supplies, including liquid glycerin in your bottled potions and homemade snow globes, spell jars & crystal balls.

WILTON (WILTON.COM/STORE):

Online and in stores, Wilton provides a tremendous selection of supplies for cake decorating, baking, and food crafting, from food-safe markers to creatively shaped cookie cutters and bakeware.

Safety eyes and other safety buttons and beads can be purchased for use in crafts made for children under age 3.

Thanks to

All the wonderfully talented *Witch Craft* contributors and family, friends, and fans; Doogie Horner and the rest of the wickedly brilliant team at Quirk Books; miraculous designer and illustrator Alison Oliver at Sugar; photographer Steve Belkowitz; extraordinary editorial interns Jane Morley and Alexandra Bitzer; bewitching model and friend Grace Kiriakos; impromptu photographer Robyn Lee of Serious Eats and The Girl Who Ate Everything; Chris Meck and the wonderful folks at Power Plant Productions in Old City, Philadelphia; The lovely Lisa Woods of Reinhard Models; Mary and the rest of the cupcake magicians at the lovely Brown Betty Dessert Boutique in Northern Liberties; and—last but not least—Glinda the Good Witch, for teaching us how to use our witch-crafting powers for good!